Heart In Paper

Dr. Chitrisha Paul

BookLeaf Publishing

India | USA | UK

Made with ❤ on the BookLeaf Publishing Platform
www.bookleafpub.in
www.bookleafpub.com

Dedication

*To my Shonamaa, who gave me roots—
and to my parents, who gave me wings.*

Preface

There was a time when writing became my refugee—
When putting pen to page was how I survive, how I
healed. This poems were not written to *impress*, but to
express. They came in the quiet of moments, between
grief and hope, in the tender spaces where love and loss
entwine. It holds the weight of sorrow, and the delicate
strength of healing.

Each poem is a step toward wholeness— mine first, and
perhaps yours too. if you find solace in this verses, know
that you are not alone. And more than anything, I hope
you find strength here— in the space between the
sorrow, in the resilience of emotion, in the quite courage
of being human.

If you are holding this book, THANK YOU. May you find
a line that rests gently in your heart, or perhaps stirs
something awake.

Acknowledgements

This book is stitched together with moments—and the people who unknowingly helped shaping them.

To my family and friends, thank you for being part of the journey. Whether you listened to my rambling, read my drafts, or just let me be while I wrestled with words, your support meant more than I ever explain.

Through it all, my parents were my pillars—
The ones who stood by me when all else seemed uncertain. Your unwavering belief in me, when I could not believe in myself, became the foundation on which these poems were built. This is for you Maa and Papa.

There's one person who stood beside me, someone who stood by me when things got messy, who reminded me why words matter to me. I didn't have the courage to even think of publishing my own poetry book but you showed me that I could. Thank you for your patience, your silence, and your steady belief in me, so much of this book is because of you.

Many of these poems were born from real life events— some mine, some shared with others. To those who lived these stories with me: Thank you. Even if you don't recognise yourself here, your impact runs deep. Your presence helped me make sense of moments I couldn't fully hold until I wrote them down.

Also a big thank you to Google you were there at 3 a.m, when my mind tangled itself in questions, in metaphors half formed. You offered definitions, poems, answers, even solace. In a strange way, you were a quiet companion in this process, and for that, I'm grateful.

But most of all, to you, the reader—this is for you. Thank you for opening this book, for choosing to spend your time inside these pages. I may never know your face, your voice, or your story— but if anything I wrote made you pause, made you feel, made you remember you are not alone— then every sleepless night and every early mornings spent writing was worth it.

You are the reason poetry lives.

The Silent Strength

Through every storm, through every fight,
You held me close, you made things right.
When dreams seemed far, when hope was thin,
You whispered softly, " you can win."

Your love, a beacon shining bright,
Guided me through the darkest night.
With every tear and every fall,
You were there to catch it all.

No words could ever truly show,
The depth of love you choose to grow.
In silence, strength was all you gave,
A love so strong, it always saved.

When I was lost, you lead me through,
With gentle hands, with heart so true.
You never doubted, never feared,
You helped me rise, when I gave up.

Your sacrifices quiet and deep,
Were promises you vowed to keep.
In every hug, in every glance,
You gave me more than just a chance.

So, here's my thanks from heart to heart,
For being with me from the start.
For being the roots, where I began,
The endless love that shapes me every day.

Dedicated to my Maa and Papa. I love you.

The Girl Who Endures

She once wore softness like the dawn,
But the world has made her carry on.
With every loss, with every tear,
She learnt to hold her heart in fear.

Yet still, beneath the hardened shell,
A tender soul begins to swell.
Though life has scared and made her tough,
Her heart remains, still soft enough.

Through every storm, through every fight,
She learnt to rise, to claim her light.
For in her depths, where pain once lay,
She stands unbroken, here to stay.

Fire And Water

You were fire— reckless, bright,
a spark that danced too close to night.
I was water— still and deep,
a tide that pulled but couldn't keep.

You scorched the air, I tried to calm,
I drowned your heart in quiet balm.
Yet every time we touched, we blurred—
Steam rose from every stolen word.

We weren't meant to last or stay—
You tried to burn, I flowed away.
But even storms remember flame,
and oceans still recall a name.

Eternal story

Beneath the moon, the pages turn,
through dark and light, our heart still yearn.
The ink may fade, the words may bend,
but love endures, it has no ends.

In shadows deep, in soft twilight,
our hearts remain in silent flight.
A tale unfolds with every kiss,
etched in the stars, forever bliss.

Fake Faces

Plastic grins in neon light,
truth dissolves in filtered night.
Eyes reflect, but never see,
the hollow hush of what could be.

Voices smooth as shattered glass,
kindness worn like fading brass.
They trade in masks, not open hands,
in this fake world, no one stands.

But just as silence filled the air,
a gaze met mine— unmasked, bare.
No words, just something softly true—
a crack of light...and it broke through.

Faded Echoes

Once, we stood in mirrored light,
our laughter soft, our hearts alight.
But threads of trust began to fray,
and silence grew where words would stay.

You turned away without a sound,
a shadow where your warmth once found.
No harsh farewell, no final fight,
just fading edges in the night.

I don't resent, I don't ask why,
just let the echoes whisper by.
A bond dissolved, too pure to keep,
now only fragments, buried deep.

Petals Of Time

Like flowers kissed by morning's glow,
we rise and stretch, we start to grow.
With colours bright, we chase the light,
yet in the dark, we fade from sight.

Each petals falls, a story told,
in moments soft, in moments bold.
But in our loss, we leave behind,
the seeds of life, of love, of time.

We bloom, we break, but never bow,
for even in death, we'll stand somehow.
Life, like flowers, comes and goes,
but in our fall, the garden grows.

Betrayal's Mark

I gave you my trust,
but you gave me lies.
Like a shadow,
your love slipped away,
unseen,
until the truth burned through.

I remember the days
before I knew -
when we were whole,
when your touch felt real.
Now, I only feel the cold,
the space you left
where warmth once lived.

You've gone,
but your betrayal lingers,
etched into the silence,
a wound I can't erase.
You left me here,

with nothing but the truth -
a love that was never real,
and a heart that must rebuild.

Brick by brick, I'll face the dawn,
for in this ache, a strength has grown.
I'll weave from sorrow a tapestry bright,
finding peace in the shadows of night.

Embrace The Now

In every breath, a world to find,
in every pause, peace for the mind.
The smallest smile the softest touch,
reminds us life can mean so much.

Even in shadows, light can grow,
in fleeting moments, we can know
the truth that whispers, calm and clear:
joy lives in all, when we are here

Sweet Like First

It hit like sun on freckled skin,
a grin too wide, a laugh too thin.
Like running barefoot through the grass,
or notes we passed in homeroom class.

Your eyes were black, or maybe brown,
the kind of look you want to lock up.
We didn't kiss— just brushed too near,
and somehow everything felt so clear.

Like watermelon in July,
a sweetness I could not deny.
So new, so wild, it made me spin,
a world beginning from within.

And though it faded, like a song,
too sweet, too young to last too long.
That kind of love still softly stays—
a light that warms the quiet days.

Falling Leaves

We are the leaves that softly fall,
not lost, but answering the call.
From vibrant green to amber gold,
we shed our past, and let it fold.

The wind, a whisper, sets us free,
as we release what used to be.
Not an end, but quiet change,
a turning point, serene, and strange,

In every fall, a chance is born,
a final bow, a soft adorn.
And though we touch the earth below,
we rise again in winds we'll know.

Awake Again

When the road is long, and the night feels too wide,
remember— the stars burn bright where the shadows
hide.
You carry light, even when it's hard to see,
strength lives within you, where it's meant to be.

Though storms may rage and winds may hawl,
You stand tall, with silence of the owl.
There's no shame in scars, no defeat in the fight,
For even broken wings will one day take flight.

Hold on through the fears, through the doubt and the
ache,
The Dawn will break, and you will find your way.
The world may bend you, but it cannot break—
For the soul that rises will always awake.

The Silent Hours

The sky draws close, a secret is kept,
while stars awake, from day they've slept.
The night unveils what they won't show,
a place for truth we long to know.

In shadows deep, we drop our guise,
revealing hearts, no need for lies.
The moon, a guide through darkened air,
shows us the path when none is there.

In stillness quiet, we find release,
our whispered words, bring inner peace.
For night is when we're truly seen,
where silent souls find space in between.

Sinking

I did not fall—
I dissolved.
No crash, no chaos,
just the soft unravelling
of a self too tired to hold its shape.

The works did not notice
when so began to fade.
There was no thunder,
no gasp of air,
only silence growing thicker
than breath.

I am deeper now than language
part the past of pain
that needs a name.

Here, gravity feels kind
it asks nothing but surrender.
No struggle, no surface,

no need to be seen.

And yet something in me watches,
still flickering like a flame
under glass, beneath a sea
that has never known fire.

Is that a hope?
or just the lost illusion?
who once believed
they could float?

When The Sky Smiled

The sky wore silver on its skin,
and joy came quietly drifting in.
A hush, a hush— then sudden light,
that kissed the leaves and danced in flight

The air grew soft, the world stood still,
as laughter bloomed on windowsills.
Bare feet found songs in puddled ground,
when silence used to be the sound.

No storm, no weight— just something new,
a sweetness in the morning dew.
And hearts, like flowers, raised their heads,
to drink what every moment said.

So let the sky be pale or bright,
there's joy in shade as much as light.
Some days, delight arrives unseen—
on clouds that glow, in silver green.

A Beam Of Light

A beam of light cut through the gray,
A golden breath where shadows lay.
It slipped through cracks in time and stone,
A silent flame, a world alone.

It danced on dust, it kissed the air,
A hush of wonder everywhere.
Not merely sun, nor distant star,
But something holy—come from far.

It did not speak, it did not stay,
But lit the soul, then slipped away.
And in its path, the dark withdrew—
A fleeting glimpse of something true.

She Wasn't Born Brave

She wasn't born brave, or bold, or loud,
Just a quiet soul, lost in the crowd.
With eyes full of wonders, heart open wide,
soft in spirit with nothing to hide.

She believed in love that wouldn't fade,
in gentle words and promises made.
But life, as it does, came rough and fast,
and taught her nothing soft will last.

The world, too heavy for hands so small,
taught her to rise each time she'd fall.
She held in tears no one could see,
and learned to smile silently.

She felt again, and once again,
and stitched herself through every pain.
Not louder, no—but firmer still,
with softer edges, stronger will.

She found her voice though it came slow,
a quiet thunder, a steady glow.
And learned that strength wears many skins—
not just the loudest one that wins.

She walks now not to prove her place,
but to honour every step she's faced.
No crown, no stage, no loud acclaim,
Just peace in knowing she overcame.

She wasn't born brave, but day by day,
she became the fire that lights her way.
And every women holds that flame—
a story whispered in her name.

Letting Go

I will not cling to what has flown,
Nor chase the echo down the hall.
Some doors are meant to close alone,
And not all rises fear the fall.

I loved, I lost, and I withstood—
The storm, the silence, all they gave.
Not every ending ends for good,
But some are meant to teach, not save.

What leaves may leave without my hand,
I do not beg, I do not bind.
True grace is learning where to stand,
And not what you must leave behind.

So here I am, both scarred and whole,
With nothing left I need to prove.
The past may mark, but not control—
I let it go, and let me move.

Woven By Wonder

In the quiet dawn,
a flower stretches its arms to the sun,
each petal a masterpiece
crafted by time's gentle hand.

The sky, a canvas of changing hues,
paints the evening in strokes of gold,
while rivers carve their secrets
into the heart of the earth,
whispering stories of ages untold.

Mountains rise in silent grace,
their peaks brushed with the breath of the wind,
and in the soft hum of nature's song,
we find beauty not in perfection,
but in the quiet imperfection of being.

You Never Knew

You took the seat, just one ahead,
while I sat quiet, cheeks flushed red.
A senior, calm, with windswept hair—
and me, behind you, barely there.

We played that game, you took your turn,
sang some old song, made my cheeks burn.
I laughed along, you caught my eye—
not long enough to ask me why?

We shared a view through foggy glass,
the trees, the sky, the towns we'd pass.
I wished you'd turn and maybe see,
the way your presence altered me.

You slept, head tilted, unaware
that every glare had stripped me bare.
I watched, in awe, this boy so free—
and whispered secret silently

The trip moved on, the days flew past,
you left, like seniors do— too fast.
You never knew, you never guessed,
that on that bus, my heart confessed.

The Midnight Spark

It came without a sound or name,
no lightning flash, no burst of flame.
Just breath, then pulse beneath the skin—
The cosmos folded deep within.

The night looked on with soft surprise,
as stardust stirred in newborn eyes.
Not loud, not large— but infinite,
an universe in candlelight.

What Was My Fault?

She sits where silence holds its breath,
between the echoes of what's left.
A thousand thoughts, a single thread:
"What was my fault?" She softly said.

He promised truth, and wore a mask,
she gave her all— was that her task?
To be the loyal, quiet light,
while he betrayed her in the night?
She wasn't blind— she chose to trust,
but watched it all turn into dust.

The walls were kind, the voices dear,
yet shadows found a way in here.
Not every bruise is born of fists—
Some hurt hides deep where no one lists,
words like knives, and doors like shields—
How do you heal in battleground fields?

The world demands she climb, achieves,

with every breath she must believe.
That dreams means more than sleepless night,
That worth is tied to silent fights.
But what of rest? Of breaking slow?
Off all the things she'll never show?

"Was it too much to trust, to try?
too much to hope, to laugh, to cry?"
She folds beneath what no one sees—
A girl still bending on her knees.

But in that ache, a pulse remains,
a quiet rage beneath the chains.
Not yet a roar— but not the same—
A spark survives inside the flame.

In The Rain, I Find You

They fall like thought we never say,
and wash the silent pain away.
The scent of rain on thirsty ground,
brings back a love I thought I'd drowned.

It smells like you— like soft goodbyes,
like winds that hush but never lie.
It stirs the soul, it breaks me through,
for every storm still smells like you.

They trace the glass with tender grace,
like fingers longing for a face.
Each drop, a word we left unsaid,
still lingers where our moments bled.

The clouds may shift, the sun may rise,
but rain still falls from aching skies.
And in its scent, I'm taken back—
to holding you, to all I lack.

So when it rains, I breathe it in,
and feel you close beneath my skin.
For love like ours, though torn in two,
Returns each time the skies turn blue.

Too Beautiful To Stay

They fell, not faded— not yet dry,
still blushing like a lover's sign.
No rot, no bruise, no time— worn scar—
just perfect ... lying where they are.

They could've crowned the tallest tree,
a fluttering badge of majesty.
But wind, or chance, or fate said no—
and beauty tumbled down below.

Look there— so bright against the dust,
too whole for loss, too soft to rust.
The kind of bloom you'd stop to praise,
if only trees got second plays.

Do petals weep for what they miss?
The honeyed sun, the morning bliss?
Or do they laugh, a little proud,
to stand out better on the ground.

They weren't too weak, or dull, or wrong—
just victims of a different song.
Not every fall is fair or true—
But still, the fallen catch the view.

When Eyes Were Enough

I love you in silence, soft as a sigh,
when glances were letters we dared not reply.
A brush of the sleeve was a thunderous thing,
and laughter together felt close to a wing.

Your name on my lips was a secret I kept,
tucked under my breath, where the butterflies slept.
You looked at the floor, I looked at the sky,
too shy to say, "Hello!", too young to ask, "Why?"

No texts, no late calls, no hearts made of screens,
just notes in desks, and half finish dreams.
We spoke through the echoes of books we had read,
through poems half- whispered and blushes we fled.

The world was much slower, our hearts even more,
yet mine raced each time you walked through the door.
I never held hands, but I still held my breath,
each time you came near felt like cheating on death.

We loved like a song hummed under the rain,
unspoken, untouched, but never in vain.
And though you moved on, and I stayed behind,
that love, shy and small, still visits my mind.

She Never Left

The winds remembers what time let decay,
your name in the plaster, worn soft and away.
Evening drapes silence on rust— eaten nails,
where laughter once lingered and memory pales.

You walk through the hush of a room with no past,
each echo a riddle, each shadow held fast.
A portrait half- charred, a letter unsent—
what's buried in walls was never content.

"The dust never knew me," you whisper, then turn,
yet footprints remain where old hungers still burn.
You swore he was gone, like a storm out at sea—
But love does not vanish, it waits patiently.

The garden, though weary, still trembles in bloom,
hope clings to the trellis, mistaking its doom.
A vine climbs the window with desperate grace,
still searching for light in a long- forsaken place.

The mirror is blank- no reflection, no face.
You sip from a chalice engraved with disgrace.
Denial is quiet, with soft, velvet walls,
a dream that persists long after it falls.

Not Enough

She sank in thoughts too sharp, too deep,
where silence sang and none would weep.
They shaped her worth with broken scales,
In whispered loves and silent fails.

Too much, too little— never just right,
she vanished quiet, out of sight.
A girl unloved, though full of grace,
lost in a world that gave no place.

She burned with fire they chose to snuff,
a soul of gold deemed not enough.
If only hearts could truly see—
She was the storm, the song, the sea.

The Empty Diary

Once, the pages spoke in haste,
a life poured out, no thought to waste.
Each word a promise, each line a tear,
a diary filled with hope and fear.

But now, the pages lie unturned,
a quiet ache, a love unearned.
What once was full, now cold and bare—
A story ended, lost in air.

The owner, too, has lost her way,
once burning bright, now lost to shame.
Her heart, once full, now cold and still,
no more to write, no more to fill.

Irony stirs in empty space—
For both the book and soul's erased.
A life once lived, now mute, untrue—
What once was full, now just like you.

After The Heat

The sun blazed on, relentless, strong,
its warmth a weight, a bitter song.
The earth, parched, cracked beneath its gaze,
a heart worn thin, lost in the blaze.

But then, the rain— soft, gentle, pure—
A whispered balm, a gentle cure.
Like healing tears that fall unseen,
washing away what might have been.

The storm inside began to fade,
as droplets kissed the scars it made.
A soul, once burning with desire,
now soothed by rain, it's aching fire.

And so, like earth, we too are freed—
from burning pain to softer need.
For after heat, the heart will find.
That rain can ease the restless mind.

What Time Forgot

I wander back through winds of time,
where laughter chimed like nursery rhyme.
A world once bright, unbound, and wide,
now flickers faintly, just outside.

The swing still sways in silent breeze,
its whispers rooted in the trees.
Were those sweet days a waking dream,
or sunlight caught in memory's stream.

Barefoot joys and skies so blue—
They fade, yet somehow still feel true.
Though grown up roads run hard and long,
I hum their tune— a distant song.

Illusion, maybe— but not gone.
It lingers when the world moves on—
not lost, just softened by the years,
A smile behind a veil of tears.

What Years Forgot To Say

The clocks all speak in measured breath,
of life, of love, of quiet death.
We choose the hours, swift and thin,
yet miss the place where we begin.

I've watch the young with eyes on fire,
hearts full of want, and want of wire.
They climb their dreams with broken grace,
not knowing time reshapes the face.

We dress in words we never mean,
like "I'm just fine", or "I've been seen."
But truth lies deep in muted tones—
in empty chairs and aging bones.

A smile can mask a thousand wars,
fought in the dark, behind close doors.
And strength is not in what we show,
but in the things we'll never know.

I've learned that silence has its place,
that not all pain must leave a trace.
And even stars, though burned and gone,
still lend their light to carry on.

So let me age without regret,
for youth is gold we often bet.
But wisdom walks, not runs away—
It stays when all else fades to grey.

Misread

I speak in shades they've never known,
but they respond in lighter tone.
They see the smile, not the ache,
mistake my silence for mistake.

They love the calm, avoid the storm,
they praise the shape, not how I form.
I bend to fit, I dim my flame,
and slowly lose my truest name.

Among the close, I feel most far—
A fading light behind a star.
Still, I would trade a thousand days
to just be held— and not explained.

The Time I Left Behind

If I could steal a thread from time,
unravel all the years I've climbed.
I'd slip into the space once known,
and taste the air where seeds were sown.

I'd speak in colours never seen,
rewind the hours that used to gleam,
the moments carved in softest stone,
where silence spoke, and hearts had grown.

I'd trade the clocks, the ticking hands,
for barefoot days on golden sands,
I'd hear the songs I let slip by,
and steal the stars from midnight sky.

I'd walk through halls, where echoes lived,
and find the love I choose to give—
But didn't, couldn't, lost in flight,
chasing ghosts that fade with night.

Yet time, she laughs in whispered tones,
a pulse inside our skin and bones.
I can't go back, though I may yearn—
for every moment, shapes who I've become.

Reborn

You loved me like a morning sun,
Not all at once— but one by one,
you warmed the parts I kept in shade,
where trust had withered, bruised and frayed.

You spoke in touch, in breath, in gaze,
unravelled me in quiet ways.
You saw the child behind my eyes—
the one who learned that love just lies.

But you—
You held me like a whispered prayer,
with hands so patient, strong and rare.
You never asked for more than "stay",
and somehow, that just let the way.

You wrapped me in a world so still,
where love was not a test of will.
No sharp demands, no games to play,
just peace in how you'd softly stay.

You brushed the dust off all I hid,
and saw the light beneath the lid.
You made me feel— a wonder, new—
that I was safe just being true.

And now I bloom, because you stayed,
because you loved the mess I made.
Because you saw what none could see—
a heart reborn, and finally free.

9 789370 925083